Discover Nests

by Juliana O'Neill

© 2018 by Juliana O'Neill
ISBN: 978-1-5324-0924-0
eISBN: 978-1-5324-0923-3
Images licensed from Fotolia.com and Adobe Stock
All rights reserved.
No portion of this book may be reproduced without
express permission of the publisher.
First Edition
Published in the United States by
Xist Publishing
www.xistpublishing.com
PO Box 61593 Irvine, CA 92602

2

Nests are homes for many animals.

Birds live in nests.

Birds build nests from grass or sticks.

Sometimes, birds use mud to make nests.

Birds lay their eggs in nests.

Baby birds must stay in the nest until they learn how to fly.

Hummingbird nests are very small.

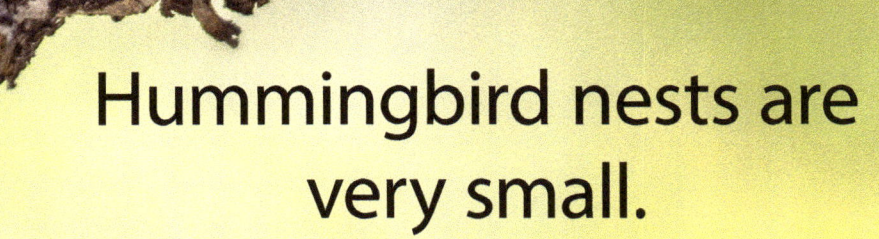

Eagle nests are very large.

Other animals also live in nests.

Alligators build nests on the ground.

Squirrels build nests in trees.

Wasps build nests up high.

Rabbits build nests under the ground.

Termite nests can rise above the ground.

There are many different kinds of nests.

31

www.ingramcontent.com/pod-product-compliance
Lightning Source LLC
LaVergne TN
LVHW010317070426
835507LV00026B/3441